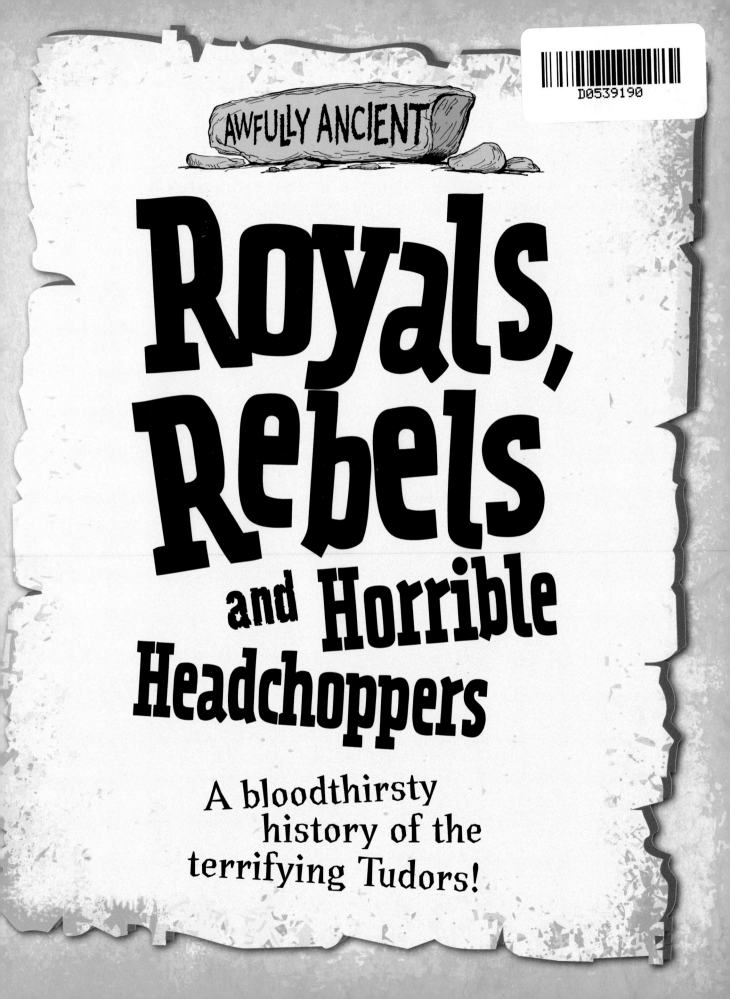

AWFULLY ANCIENT

Royals, Rebels and Horrible Headchoppers

A bloodthirsty history of the terrifying Tudors!

First published in 2014 by Wayland

Copyright © Wayland 2014

Wayland
338 Euston Road
London
NW1 3BH

Wayland Australia
Level 17/207 Kent Street
Sydney NSW 2000

Senior editor: Julia Adams
Illustrator: Tom Morgan-Jones
Designer: Rocket Design (East Anglia) Ltd

Dewey classification: 364'.09-dc23

ISBN 978 0 7502 7989 5
E-book ISBN 978 0 7502 9370 9

Printed in China
10 9 8 7 6 5 4 3 2 1

Wayland is a division of Hachette Children's
Books, an Hachette UK company.
www.hachette.co.uk

What's this shifty looking
character up to?
Find out on page 11

Too young for a real
horse? Then why not
saddle up one of these?
See page 12...

Would 'sir' like a side order of scurvy
with his dried cod and dried peas? Read
all about meals at sea on page 24.

Contents

Chopped off hands and feet? A heart bleeding into a cup? See p. 10 for explanations...

A book about the Tudors wouldn't be complete without the Bard.

From 1485 to 1603, England was ruled by the Tudor dynasty: one family that held on to power for 118 years. They won the throne in a bloodthirsty battle and were ready to use force to keep it.

The message was: Don't mess with the Tudors!

Richard III (reigned 1483–1485)

Richard was the last Plantagenet king. He was killed at the Battle of Bosworth in 1485 fighting the armies of Henry Tudor. This was the last battle of the Wars of the Roses a struggle that had lasted over 30 years.

Henry VII (reigned 1485–1509)

Henry strengthened the hold of the Tudors by marrying Elizabeth of York, uniting the Lancaster and York families.

Henry VIII (reigned from 1509–1547

Henry was desperate for a son and was always short of money. He tried to solve both problems by divorcing Catherine of Aragon, taking over the Catholic Church and setting up the Protestant Church of England.

Edward VI (reigned 1547–1553)

Edward was only nine when he became King. Edward and

his advisers kept the Church of England but tragically Edward died when he was only 15.

Mary I (reigned 1553–1558)

Mary tried to bring back Catholicism and married King Philip of Spain (the leading Catholic Country). Hundreds of Protestants were burned at the stake.

Elizabeth I (reigned 1558–1603)

Elizabeth tried to end fights over religion, but faced several Catholic plots to overthrow her. England became a great trading nation and sea power. The navy was able to fight off the mighty Spanish Armada in 1588.

Right Royal Deaths

Even kings and queens didn't live long in Tudor times

Richard III Killed by blows to the head with a halberd, aged 33

Henry VII Died of tuberculosis, aged 52

Henry VIII Died of kidney and liver failure, aggravated by huge leg ulcers, aged 55

Edward VI Died of tuberculosis, aged just 15, but rumours said he was poisoned

Mary I Died during a flu epidemic, but had ovarian cancer too, aged 42

Elizabeth I Possibly died from blood poisoning caused by her lead-based make up, aged 69

Some may argue that Edward VI was a little young for the throne...

Monasteries and Martyrs

In 16th century Europe, everyone was Christian, but they were having one VERY BIG argument – are you a Catholic or Protestant Christian? People were prepared to die to defend their beliefs.

Religious revolution

Now read carefully, this bit is complicated:

At first, Henry VIII was a devout Catholic. The Pope even gave him the title *Defender of the Faith* – the Catholic faith. But in 1529, the Pope refused to grant Henry a divorce from his first wife, Catherine of Aragon. Henry was so furious he decided to break away from the Catholic Church. In 1533, Henry made himself head of the new Church of England, divorced Catherine and married Anne Boleyn. This upheaval is called the Reformation – and among the big losers were the monasteries.

Monasteries

The monasteries were communities of monks and nuns, some of them very wealthy. To make sure they didn't back the Pope – and to get his hands on their money – Henry plotted to shut them down.

Between 1536 and 1540, about 850 monasteries were seized by Henry's officials. More than 12,000 monks and nuns were forced to leave, but most were given pensions, so they wouldn't join rebellions against the King. Monastery lands and buildings were rented cheaply to nobles who supported Henry.

A roasting

Henry paid off all his debts with money from the monasteries, but set off years of strife. His eldest daughter, Queen Mary, tried to bring back Catholicism. A shocking 283 Protestants who refused to change were burnt at the stake during her short reign.

'Sizzle'

That'll teach 'em!

TERRIFYING TUDORS
Vicious vandalism

England's monasteries are tourist attractions now – for example Fountains Abbey in Yorkshire. But why are they all ruins?

- Jewels, gold and silver were seized and sent to the Royal treasury.
- Lead was ripped from roofs and melted down, letting the rain pour in.
- Libraries of precious manuscripts were looted and some even used as rag.s
- Wood and glass were stripped out to use in nearby homes.
- Walls were torn down for building stone.

Result – Instant Ruins

Wilful Wives

Henry VIII wanted his wives to love, honour and obey him. But he was in for a right royal shock.

WIFE 1 Catherine of Aragon 1485–1536

Catherine was a Spanish princess. She married Prince Arthur in 1501, but sadly he died six months later. In 1509, she was married to Henry, and at first they were blissfully happy. Catherine had six children, including two boys — but only Mary survived. Eager for a son, Henry married Anne Boleyn in secret in January 1533 and divorced Catherine in May.

WIFE 2 Anne Boleyn 1501–1536

Anne Boleyn was the lady-in-waiting for Catherine. She caught the eye of the King, and by 1527 he was madly in love with her. However, there was one slight problem for Henry: Anne gave birth to Elizabeth in 1533, but never gave birth to a son and heir. To get rid of Anne, she was accused of being unfaithful and beheaded.

WIFE 3 Jane Seymour 1508–1537

Jane was Henry's favourite wife. She gave birth to his only surviving son Edward — who became Edward VI. Jane died shortly after his birth.

TERRIFYING TUDORS
Going for the chop

Anne Boleyn on the day of her execution

I heard say the executioner was very good, and I have a little neck.

WIFE 4 | Anne of Cleves
1515–1557

Henry married Anne because she was a German Princess from a Protestant country. But he didn't like her from the start. She was neither attractive to him nor musical (and Henry loved music). Anne agreed to a divorce — for a price. She became one of the wealthiest women in England.

whiff!

WIFE 6 | Catherine Parr
1512–1548

WIFE 5 | Catherine Howard
1521–1542

Catherine was 19 when she married Henry. She brought a spark back to his life, but didn't become pregnant. Enemies at court plotted her downfall and she was beheaded for having a love affair with another man.

Catherine had a successful marriage to Henry, though she had powerful enemies at court who tried to turn the King against her. Catherine supervised the education of all three of Henry's children and nursed him while he was dying — a very smelly job since he had rotting ulcers on his legs.

Riotous Rebels

Zounds!

The Pilgrims of Grace had their own flag, showing the five wounds of Christ on the Cross.

In Tudor times, ordinary people suffered famine, plague, poverty and topsy–turvy religious changes. Most of the time, they put up with their problems, but sometimes resentment boiled over into revolt.

Reasons to rebel

Most rebellions were local, and people joined in because they were angry about something happening close to home, such as the loss of a nearby monastery. Sometimes national events seemed to threaten them, such as rumours that King Philip of Spain would conquer England if he married Queen Mary.

Proud pilgrims

Most rebellions were easily defeated, but on occasions the Tudors' rule hung by a thread. The most serious rebellion was *The Pilgrimage of Grace* in 1537. More than 35,000 rebels gathered under the skilled leadership of the lawyer Robert Aske. They demanded an end to the closure of the monasteries. Henry won by trickery. He persuaded the rebels

Sneaky double crosser

Tudor rebels timeline

Name of rebellion	When?	Led by?	Where?	What did they want?
The Pilgrimage of Grace	1536	Robert Aske	Yorkshire	To save the monasteries
Kett's Rebellion	1549	Robert Kett	Norfolk	To stop the enclosure of common land by nobles
Wyatt's Rebellion	1554	Sir Thomas Wyatt	Kent	To stop the marriage of Queen Mary to King Philip of Spain
The Northern Rebellion	1569	The Earls of Westmoreland and Northumberland	Northern England	To overthrow Queen Elizabeth and replace her with Mary, Queen of Scots
Tyrone's Rebellion	1594	Irish chieftain Hugh O'Neill	Ireland, mainly Ulster	To throw out English rule

to go home by promising the monasteries would be spared. When they disbanded, their leaders were arrested and hung.

Plucky plotters

Some rebels worked in small, secret groups to bring down the Tudors. In 1586, the Babington plotters conspired to assassinate Queen Elizabeth and replace her with Catholic Mary, Queen of Scots. Elizabeth's spymaster Francis Walsingham used double agents to expose their plans, and the plotters were tortured and executed for treason.

A top Tudor spymaster

A Tudor Childhood

Zounds!

Tudor children often drank beer – brewing kills germs and made beer safer to drink than milk or water.

Being born a Tudor was tough. One in four children died before their first birthday and over half before they were 10. Some babies died during birth, while others perished from infections such as infant diarrhoea, caused by contaminated food or water. Accidents took their toll, too. Toddlers, often left to roam by busy mothers, died falling in open fires, drowning in ponds or were trampled by farm animals.

Terrific toys

Not surprisingly, surviving children were treasured. Most were brought up in small families, much like our own, by loving parents. They had great toys made out of cheap everyday materials: balls from clay wrapped in cloth; hobby horses and swords from wood, whistles and pea-shooters from reeds.

A favourite game was knucklebones: throw five bones (the small ankle bones of sheep) in the air and catch as many as possible on the back of your hand. Boys and girls wore the same kind of clothes; usually loose fitting dresses until they were around the age of seven, when boys were breeched – given their first pair of breeches to show they were young men.

Grinding grammars

If parents could afford it, boys were sent to the local grammar school to be taught maths, reading, writing and Latin. Girls stayed at home and learned how to run a home. For the boys, school days lasted from

Imagine prancing about with your chums on one of these...

12

6am to 5pm and teachers were super strict. Naughty pupils were beaten with a birch cane and boys who talked back were sometimes struck on the mouth with a flat stick that looked like a ruler.

Ah, the good old pea-shooter. Great fun in the classroom (don't get caught, though!).

Knucklebones

Ooooo!

Aaaah!

TERRIFYING TUDORS

Perilous play

Coroners' inquests tell us about the misfortunes of some Tudor children.

Date	Name	Age	Where?	Cause of death
17 May 1569	Lord George Dacre	7	Thetford	The wooden vaulting horse he was playing on collapsed and crushed his head
12 June 1552	Edmind Fenwycke	8	Newcastle upon Tyne	Killed while watching a play. A gun used for special effects exploded and a fragment hit his head.
18 July 1554	John Malkyn	12	Great Missenden	Drowned chasing a moorhen in the moat of Missenden Abbey
24 July 1559	Catherine Brewis	7	Hertford	Tried to walk across the River Lea on a beam, fell reaching for a floating twig and drowned.

Plague Streets

Woah, even the doctors were scary!

Towns grew fast in Tudor times and sanitation was... well, stinky. People moved away from the countryside, looking for work, and urban populations jumped. London was by far the biggest city and grew from around 75,000 people in 1485 to 225,000 in 1603. The next largest was Bristol, growing from 10,000 people to 20,000 in the same period.

TERRIFYING TUDORS

Plague rats

The plague was spread by fleas that lived on black rats. They were also called house rats, because they like living near people and all that tasty rubbish! The rats caught the plague too and when they died – guess what the fleas did? After three days of living on a dead rat, they were pretty hungry, so they jumped onto a nice, blood-filled human.

Reeking rubbish

Whatever their size, Tudor towns were squalid. There were no drainage systems and human and animal poo was dumped in the street or kept in piles, called middens. And then there was the rubbish...

Reeking waste from homes and workshops choked the narrow streets: rotting vegetables; broken pots and bottles; offal from butchers and leather scraps from shoemakers. A Tudor rubbish dump found in 1999 near Potters Field in London even had a banana skin!

The terrible state of Tudor towns attracted thousands of rats.

Pesky Plague

These filthy conditions made the perfect breeding ground for the plague. Epidemics swept through England every few years, killing thousands of people. Southampton was hit badly in 1563 and again in 1581, wiping out more than 10 per cent of the population. In 1579, Newcastle suffered even more, with 2,000 dead — one in five of all inhabitants.

The symptoms of the plague were shocking. Flea bites caused huge swellings called *bubos*, usually in the groin, on the thigh, in an armpit or on the neck. Hence the name 'bubonic plague'. The infection took three to five days for people to become ill and another three to five days to kill. Three quarters of those who caught the plague died.

Plague suspects were locked in their homes and guarded by watchmen to stop them leaving — a basic system of quarantine. Doctors tried herbal remedies or bleeding their victims with leeches, but nothing worked. Many families fled the stricken towns to live with relatives in the country — carrying the fleas and the plague with them.

Ah, the good old days...

Typical Tudor Street
(Duck! There's some poo coming your way!)

Creepy Crimes and Criminals

Many crimes in Tudor times were much the same as today, such as murder, theft and fraud. Other offences seem strange to modern eyes. Arguing with neighbours — a crime called barratry — was seen as really bad behaviour, while not going to church on Sunday meant a fine of up to £20 a month — a huge sum.

Unlucky lawman

The Tudors didn't have a police force. Local Justices of the Peace (JPs), usually important landowners and nobles, kept law and order. Serious crimes, such as murder and robbery, were tried at Assize courts held twice a year in every county.

The pillory

Loser!

Ha ha!

16

A travelling judge

Travelling judges, appointed by the monarch, heard cases and held the power of life or death.

Punishments and penalties

Punishments were meant to deter criminals, so many were very harsh. Traitors faced the worst fate — they were hanged, drawn and quartered. This meant they were hanged till nearly dead and then their stomachs were slashed open and their intestines pulled out. Finally, their hopefully dead bodies were chopped into four pieces.

Murderers and many robbers were just hung — but death was slow because they choked to death. Petty criminals, such as beggars, could be whipped, branded or even have a hand amputated. Milder penalties included putting the offender in the pillory and reading out their crimes to the public.

That's criminal talk

Tudor criminals had a secret language, with words for each kind of crook. Here are a few:

ABRAHAM MAN

A beggar who pretends to be insane, so people take pity and give more money.

CONEY-CATCHER

A thief who robs through trickery — for example gambling with loaded dice.

PRIGGER OR PRANCER

A horse thief.

HIGH LAWYER

A highwayman.

NIP

A thief who cut purses with a knife.

Nay.

Move!

SCRIPPER

A look-out for a highwayman.

FOIST

A pickpocket.

Food and Famine

People thought that uncooked fruit and veg spread diseases, so lots of stuff was boiled to mush.

The population of Tudor England grew from around 2.5 million in 1500 to around 4 million in 1600 — a huge increase. One of the greatest achievements of the age was growing enough food to feed all these extra mouths — or at least trying to...

Dull diet

Most Tudors were famers or smallholders and lived in the countryside. They kept a few animals, especially pigs, and grew their own crops. The main foods were coarse, grey bread, made from rye or barley, and vegetables such as turnips, onions and beans.

Surprisingly, people were suspicious of eating uncooked vegetables because they believed this caused diseases! Even fruit was suspect, and during the plague outbreak of 1569, selling fresh fruit was against the law.

Tudor pigs looked like wild boars and slaughtering one was a busy family event. Every part of the animal was eaten or used in some way: the carcass was cut into joints, such as hams and pork bellys; the blood made nutritious puddings; the fat was made into lard; the innards into sausage skins and the bristles were used — to make brushes.

Zounds!

Remember: potatoes, tomatoes and chocolate were new crops from the Americas and only grown by a few rich people as a curiosity.

Oooh, look! A new brush!

Oink

Foul famine

If harvests were good, so was life. But bad weather and rising prices brought famine and even starvation. The worst years lasted from 1594 to 1598. The government ordered merchants to stop hoarding grain and bakers to make bread from the cheapest flour, so that even the poorest people could buy a loaf. Nevertheless, thousands died — 25 bodies were cleared from the streets of Newcastle alone in the autumn of 1597.

TERRIBLE TUDORS

Pleasing pottage

Most Tudor people weren't rich and ate one cooked meal a day — pottage or soup. What went in it depended on the time of year. So this is your chance to eat like a Tudor...

Method:

- Fetch water from the river or well.

- Put it in your cauldron and light the fire under it. (OK, since it's you — use the tap and a pan.)

- Make a stock with whatever you have: onions; carrots; leeks; cabbage; dried beans; left-over scraps of meat.

- Season with traditional English herbs: thyme; sage; parsley; marjoram; rosemary.

- Add porridge oats — the more you add, the thicker the pottage.

Enjoy!

Mad Medicines

Tudor doctors believed there were four humours present in a person's body – Earth, Air, Fire and Water. If someone was sick, it was because the humours had become unbalanced. The doctor's job was to diagnose the imbalance and put it right.

Bloomin' bleeding

The main Tudor treatments weren't fun for the patient — purges to make them poo or be sick; using leeches to drain 'impure' blood or, more drastically, bleeding a patient by cutting a vein. Thankfully, more enlightened doctors realised the importance of simple cures, such as rest, diet, exercise and fresh air.

Poor Tudors couldn't afford doctors, so they went to apothecaries (chemists) for drugs, or to local healers (a bit like witch doctors) for remedies. Often the prescriptions were based on magic, superstition or old wives' tales – including the 'tricky treatments' opposite.

Powerful potions

Medicines made from plants, however, could be quite effective. Flowers called foxgloves were recommended for steadying the pulse or heart rate and feverfew was used for headaches, while comfrey and liquorice were administered for bronchitis. Most large Tudor houses had herb gardens, so wealthy housewives could grow the ingredients and make their own family medicines.

The best doctors were surgeons. Many gained experience treating war wounds, so they had a detailed knowledge of human anatomy.

Operations were performed without anaesthetics or antiseptics, though opium was used to make a patient drowsy and sour wine was applied to clean wounds. Treating injuries such as broken limbs was reasonably safe, but any operation that involved deep incisions risked infection and death through blood poisoning.

Here we see a Tudor chap being completely cured of his deafness... not!

Ah, the Tudor chemist. Most of the medicine was made up of dead animals...

Ailment: Headache
Treatment: Take a lock of your hair, boil it in your wee and throw it on the fire. If this does not work, press a hangman's rope to your head.

Ailment: Deafness
Treatment: Take the gall bladder (an organ that is part of the digestive system) of a hare and the grease of a fox. Warm the mixture and place in the ear.

Ailment: Toothache
Treatment: Go thrice about the churchyard.

TUDOR APOTHECARY

Rub this in, sir. That rash should be completely gone by the morning...

Wise Men and Witches

The Tudors were deeply superstitious. Even Queen Elizabeth I had a royal astrologer at court, Dr John Dee. He suggested the date for her coronation to bring good fortune to her reign, and spent many years experimenting with alchemy (trying to turn lead into gold).

Wicked witches

Nearly everyone believed in God, angels and the power of good.

But the bible also taught that evil was the work of the devil and his servants — witches and warlocks. If something went wrong — the death of a child; an illness in the family or a cow no longer giving milk — the victims blamed witches. Suspicion usually fell on anyone with a reputation for using magic — usually a poor, older woman who scratched a living selling charms and potions.

TERRIBLE TUDORS

Fiery signs

The fire was the centre of every Tudor home, and people believed flames had magic powers. Watching the fire was more exciting than TV!

Spitting on the flames – this was done for good luck.

Spitting on a hot cinder – if it crackled, you would become rich. (In which case, we're not sure why all Tudors weren't wealthy...)

Cinder jumped out of the fire – sign that there was a new birth on the way.

Coals burning in a hollow heap – sign that a parting would soon occur.

Fire wouldn't burn – Uh oh, something evil was close by.

Terrifying trials

Even so, it took a while for the English to get excited about witchcraft. There were no witch trials in early Tudor times, although thousands of people were being arrested and burned on mainland Europe. It wasn't until 1542 that Henry VIII passed the first law making it a crime to use 'witchecraftes, enchauntementes or sorceries' to harm people.

Court records show that most Tudor witch trials — around 270 — took place during the reign of Elizabeth I. Of those accused, 243 were women and just 23 men. Essex seemed to be a witch hotspot, with 178 people put on trial — 159 of them women. Of these, 111 were found not guilty, and 58 were executed. Two unlucky suspects died of the plague in prison.

On trial

Gulp!

Aha! An old woman with a cat. You MUST be guilty!

All at Sea

Help!

Zounds!

Amazingly, most Tudor sailors couldn't swim. If the ship sank, so did they!

England became a seafaring nation during the 16th century. Overseas trade boomed, Tudor explorers set out across the world and a powerful navy fought off invaders.

Tudor trade

In early Tudor times, England only had around 5,000 experienced sailors — fewer than the number of priests. Most trade was with France and the Low Countries — modern Holland and Belgium. Merchants traded wool and woollen cloth.

Enterprising Explorers

By 1600, England was an emerging world power. Tudor explorers were late in the game, compared to the Spanish, but made up for lost time. Francis Drake sailed a fleet around the world from 1577 to 1580. He was the first European to reach California and plundered Spanish colonies and ships on his way.

Starting slavery

In the 1560s, John Hawkins, with the backing of Queen Elizabeth I, started the bloodthirsty English slave trade. He sold cloth to African chiefs in exchange for slaves, sold the slaves in the Caribbean to work on plantations and took cargoes of fish back to England.

Suffering sailors

English sailors had hard lives. They were away from port for months or even years. Wages were poor and injured sailors were left to beg on the streets. Most food on long voyages was preserved — salted beef or pork, dried cod and dried peas. This diet led to scurvy, a disease caused by lack of vitamin C. Symptoms included black and blue blotches on the skin and bleeding gums.

TERRIBLE TUDORS

Exciting explorers

Date	Explorers	Voyage	Results
1497	John Cabot	Discovered a 'new found land': Newfoundland in Canada.	Cabot found rich fishing grounds.
1553	Hugh Willoughby and Richard Chancellor	Tried to sail around the North of Russia.	Willoughby visited Moscow and set up trade in furs and timber.
1580s	Sir Walter Raleigh	Set up colonies in America.	Raleigh's colonies failed, but paved the way for the first successful settlement in Virginia in 1607.

Perilous Pastimes

Zounds!

Tudor-style football is still played in Ashbourne, Derbyshire, today. There are no rules and the goals are 4.5 km apart.

The Tudors worked hard — and played hard, too. Sports and pastimes were an important feature of life.

Curious customs

The passing of the year was marked by customs so old that no one could remember how they began. On May Day, people celebrated the return of spring by dancing round the maypole. In late September, a lavish harvest supper was served to workers after the corn was gathered in. The last sheaf was made into a corn dolly — a place for the female corn spirit to hide until the next growing season. The Christmas holidays lasted for 12 days. There was feasting and mummers (village players) performed the adventures of St George.

Serious sports

Tudor nobles had their own expensive sports. They fought jousts, just like medieval knights. This was a test of courage and very dangerous — even for kings. In 1536, Henry VIII was badly injured when his horse fell on top of him. More peacefully, large country houses had bowling greens or alleys and a new sport from France was catching on — 'Tenez', or tennis. At first, this was played with gloved hands, but by the mid 16th century, rackets were being used.

In 1512, a new law banned ordinary people from a whole range of games,

Do you want my racket?

Don't be ridiculous!

including tennis, dice, cards, bowls, skittles and even football. Although there was a risk of a fine, most Tudors ignored it and played on! The approved sport was archery. English archers were among the deadliest soldiers in Europe — but to kill with a bow took a lot of practise.

The way Tudors treated animals for sport seems very bloodthirsty to us nowadays. Bulls or bears were baited (chained up and made to fight ferocious dogs), while in cock fights, cockerels with metal spurs on their legs pecked and gouged each other to death.

TERRIBLE TUDORS

Foul football

Philip Stubbes wrote one of the first descriptions of football, in 1585. Sounds like fun... NOT!

As for football, it may rather be called a friendly fight. Doth not everyone lie in wait for their adversary seeking to... pitch him on his nose, though it be on hard stones or in a ditch... sometimes their necks are broken, sometimes their noses gush with blood.

Passionate Plays

The Globe theatre in London was one of the first purpose built playhouses ever.

Watching plays was popular with rich and poor alike. Sometimes ordinary people were the performers, but increasingly, the theatre offered fame and fortune to full-time playwrights and actors.

It's a mystery

Most people could not read or write so plays were a powerful way to spread ideas. Mystery plays told stories from the bible. In towns all over England, groups of workers called Guilds put on sets of plays with a religious theme every year. In Newcastle, the Tailors performed *The Descent into Hell*, while the Shipwrights enacted *Noah's Ark*.

Audiences expected spectacular special effects — bells rang, drums rolled, Christ suffered on the cross

and the devil appeared in clouds of sulphurous smoke. Eventually, mystery plays were banned for being too Catholic, but in modern times some scripts have been rediscovered. Medieval and Tudor mysteries from Wakefield and York are once again playing to huge crowds.

Proper plays

Troops of actors had toured the country for hundreds of years, performing in castles and manor halls for nobles, as well as fairs and markets for ordinary folk. But in 1576, an important change began: the first two purpose-built

It turns out after all that Richard III really was a hunchback.

Zounds!

For years, most historians reckoned that Richard III wasn't disabled in any way and that Shakespeare was just trying to please Queen Elizabeth.

BUT... Richard's skeleton was discovered by archaeologists in Leicester in 2013. The bones showed 10 battle wounds and a curved spine – he really was 'hunchbacked'.

TERRIBLE TUDORS

Ridiculing Richard

Shakespeare wrote Richard III in 1592. Remember – Richard was killed at the Battle of Bosworth by Queen Elizabeth I's grandfather, Henry VII. In this passage Shakespeare makes him seem like a deformed monster.

I that am
Cheated of feature by dissembling nature,
Deformed, unfinished, sent before my time,
Into this breathing world scare half made up
And that so lamely and unfashionable
That dogs bark at me as I halt by them.

playhouses were opened in London, and by 1600, huge crowds went to the theatre every week.

William Shakespeare, the most successful playwright of the age, wrote for a company called *The Queen's Men*. They performed at the new *Globe Theatre*, opened in 1599. As their name suggested, they had the support of Elizabeth I, but in return their plays had to show the greatness of England and the Tudor dynasty. To make sure, all new scripts, including Shakespeare's, had to be approved by the Lord Chancellor.

Glossary

adversary: enemy

anticoagulant: substance that stops blood from clotting

astrologer: someone who studies the movements of the planets and the stars, believing they have an influence on humans

Babington Plot: named after the young Catholic nobleman, Anthony Babington, one of the main conspirators of a plot to overthrow Queen Elizabeth I.

breeches: knee-length trousers

bristles: the thick hairs of a pig

Catholic: a member of the Roman Catholic Church, led by the Pope in Rome

church: a Christian building of worship

Church: a particular Christian organisation with its own places of worship and religious leader; for example, the Protestant Church

coroner's inquests: official investigations into the causes of deaths

double agents: spies who pretend to be plotters

enclosure: fenced off common land, such as moors, often to graze sheep

halbard: broad-bladed pike or spear

Lord Chancellor: leading servant of the monarch, also an important judge

mystery plays: Medieval and Tudor plays, based on bible stories

parish: the area around a church; usually a village or section of a town

Pope: head of the Catholic Church

Protestant: a Christian belonging to a Church that had broken away from the Catholic faith

smallholders: people who owned or rented a small patch of land to grow crops. They needed to carry out other jobs as well to make a living, such as weaving.

tuberculosis: a disease of the lungs; the symptoms include loss of appetite, exhaustion, lungs full of fluid and coughing up blood

urban: a built up area; a town or city

zounds!: a Tudor expression of anger and surprise; rough meaning: by God's wounds!

More information

Places to visit

Weald and Downland Open Air Museum in Chichester. This museum exhibits 600 years of life in south-east England, with original buildings, agricultural machinery, rural crafts and a collection of around 15,000 artefacts. www.wealddown.co.uk

The Golden Hinde II, London. Located on the South Bank of the River Thames, this is a full-size reconstruction of the ship Sir Francis Drake used to sail around the world between 1577 and 1580. www.goldenhinde.com

Hardwick Hall, Chesterfield. A stunning Elizabethan house built for Bess of Hardwick, Countess of Shrewsbury. It was completed in 1597 and was designed to showcase Beth's wealth and status. www.nationaltrust.org.uk/hardwick

Websites

insult.dream40.org
Have fun with this Shakespearean insult generator from the Royal Shakespeare Company. Warning: dangerous insults!

irisharchaeology.ie
Type 'toys' into the search box and read a great article about the great hoard of toys found in Market Harborough parish church.

Books

Henry VIII Build a 14-Seat Lavatory! by Kay Barnham, Wayland (2014)

The Gruesome Truth About the Tudors by Jillian Powell, Wayland (2012)

Explore! – Tudors by Jane Bingham, Wayland (2014)

Index

MORE HISTORY THAN YOU CAN SHAKE A STICK AT!

Why not find out more about the terrible Tudors, dastardly dictators and the raucous Romans with our array of humorous history titles...

TRUTH or BUSTED

WORLD WAR ONE MADE SOLDIERS' FEET GO ROTTEN!

The fact or fiction behind **BATTLES & WARS**

978 0 7502 8132 4

TRUTH or BUSTED

MEDIEVAL PEOPLE WASHED THEIR CLOTHES IN WEE!

Weeee!

The fact or fiction behind **HISTORY**

978 0 7502 6958 2

TRUTH or BUSTED

HENRY VIII BUILT A 14-SEAT LAVATORY!

The fact or fiction behind **TUDORS**

978 0 7502 8130 0

TRUTH or BUSTED

VICTORIAN WORKERS TURNED DOG POO INTO GOLD!

The fact or fiction behind **VICTORIANS**

978 0 7502 8129 4

TRUTH or BUSTED

FEMALE PHARAOHS WORE FALSE BEARDS!

The fact or fiction behind **EGYPTIANS**

978 0 7502 8133 1

TRUTH or BUSTED

WARM GLADIATOR BLOOD WAS USED AS MEDICINE!

The fact or fiction behind **ROMANS**

978 0 7502 8134 8

Barmy Biogs

BONKERS BOFFINS, INVENTORS and other Eccentric Eggheads

978 0 7502 7718 1

Barmy Biogs

CRACKPOT KINGS, QUEENS and other Daft Royals

978 0 7502 7717 4

Barmy Biogs

DASTARDLY DICTATORS, RULERS and other Loony Leaders

978 0 7502 7720 4

Barmy Biogs

POTTY PAINTERS, WRITERS and other Barmy Artists

978 0 7502 7719 8